Cozy Christmas

COLORING BOOK

JESSICA MAZURKIEWICZ

DOVER PUBLICATIONS
GARDEN CITY, NEW YORK

Relax and get cozy as you color these 31 picturesque holiday scenes that capture the joy, warmth, and comfort of Christmas. The cheerful images conjure welcoming thoughts of this festive season and feature beautifully decorated trees with piles of presents, delicious sweet treats, glowing fireplaces, and stockings "hung by the chimney with care." The images are printed on one side only, and the pages are perforated for easy removal and display of your finished artwork.

Bibliographical Note

Cozy Christmas Coloring Book is a new work,
first published by Dover Publications in 2021.

International Standard Book Number
ISBN-13: 978-0-486-84861-7
ISBN-10: 0-486-84861-2

Manufactured in the United States of America
84861201
www.doverpublications.com

2 4 6 8 10 9 7 5 3 1
2021